Adaline Talcott Emerson, Kimball Stone

Love-Bound And Other Poems

Adaline Talcott Emerson, Kimball Stone

Love-Bound And Other Poems

ISBN/EAN: 9783744705165

Printed in Europe, USA, Canada, Australia, Japan

Cover: Foto ©Thomas Meinert / pixelio.de

More available books at **www.hansebooks.com**

LOVE-BOUND
AND OTHER POEMS

BY
ADALINE TALCOTT EMERSON

PRINTED AT
THE UNIVERSITY PRESS
CAMBRIDGE, MASSACHUSETTS
MDCCCXCIV

TO
MY BLESSED HUSBAND,
THE INSPIRATION OF MY LIFE, AND THE DEAR CHILDREN, THE FRUIT OF OUR LOVE, I DEDICATE THIS VOLUME, THE OUTCOME OF MANY EXPERIENCES, THE RIPENING THOUGHT OF MANY YEARS.

A FORE-WORD AND FOR-WORD.

POETRY is, among other things, the universal expression of individual emotion. This gives verse its importance and its audacity. There is a sense in which each essay in verse challenges all the past, and enters the list with the great of all time. But there comes a season, both early and late, in all tongues, when verse is common to all. Once early, when speech is still fluid, in the days of the ballad, and once late, as in our own day, when the field of verse is once more open to all, because the seeds of rhyme have been sown in every soul. At such a time in each tongue, verse becomes the frequent resource of perthis verse, to a special circle, and some, now and then one in a century, to the world. In the just weight of worth, the last does not still the second. One

> Sings to the wide world, and she to her nest;
> In the nice ear of Nature which song is the best?

TALCOTT WILLIAMS.

PHILADELPHIA,
   September the Seventh, 1894.

A TABLE OF THE CONTENTS OF LOVE–BOUND

"LOVE-BOUND," 11
TO MY LOVE, 14
THE OFFICE, 16
LOVE'S DREAM, 17
BONDAGE, 20
COUNT THE WEEKS BY SUNDAYS, 23
SUNSHINE ON THE CHAMBER CEILING, 27
SUMMER CLOUDS, 30
SNOW-FLAKES, 31
THE SONG OF THE OCEAN, 34
ANSWER TO H. H.'S QUESTION, 38
THE ENGADINE VILLAGES, 41
SMOKE OF THE CITY, 42
THE THUNDER, 44
AUTUMN, 45
NOVEMBER, 46
TO-MORROW, 47
PICTURES, 49
THE OCEAN'S LULLABY, 51
SUNRISE ON LAKE SUPERIOR, 53
THE NIGHT WINDS, 55
STORM IN CALIFORNIA, 58
COMING SNOW-STORM, 61
SEA-SHELLS, 63
OHO! YE WINDS, 65
MOTHERHOOD, 69
THE FIRST BABY, 72
HELEN, 74
CHILDHOOD PASSING, 79
INTO YOUTH, 81
"TO A YOUNG CHILD," 83
"COUNT LIFE BY DEEDS," 85
FRIENDSHIP, 87
REVERIES, 88
SAVED, 89
REMEMBRANCE, 92
DREAMS, 94
A FRAGMENT, 95
1776–1876, 99
JAMES A. GARFIELD, 102

NUREMBERG'S GABLES, 105
THE REV. JOSEPH HAVEN, D.D., 108
TO WHITTIER, 110
FAIR DRYBURGH ABBEY, 112
COURAGE BY THE WAY, 121
GOD'S WILL, 123
THE BODY'S REST, 127
UNREST, 129
CALL FOR HELP, 130
CLING NOT TO THE PAST, 132
QUESTIONINGS, 134
IN THE END, 136
SHIELDING, 138
SHADOWS, 140
"REST FOR THE WEARY," 142
EASTER BELLS, 143
LIGHT AHEAD, 145
GUIDANCE, 147
TO MY MOTHER, 149
A FAREWELL, 151
INTO THE SILENCE, 154
WITHERED LEAVES, 157
CHRISTMAS' AMEN, 158
THE DYING YEAR, 159
HOLIDAYS OF 1873, 165
A VALENTINE, 169
LITTLE CHILDREN, 171
AN APRIL DAY, 173
BABY ADALYN, 175
BABY BELLE HINCHLIFF, 177
KISSES, 179
WATCHING FOR MAMMA, 180
TO THE LINNET, 181
THE DIAMOND NECKLACE, 183
A JINGLE, 186
LAMBKIN, 187
NATURE'S UNDERTONES, 188
THE FUTURE, 192

Not to the skillful critic,
　Nor to the public throng,
To you my inmost thoughts I bring, —
　To you my simple lays belong.

"LOVE-BOUND."

THE shy partridge calls to his loved mate,
    "More wet,"
  The nightingale sings in the fen,
The bobolink carols to all his Wee Babes,
    And sweet is the song of the wren.

The kine in the meadow, the sheep in the fold;
    The chanticleer's voice on the wind;
From each to the other sweet music we hear,
    "Oh, Love-bound are we to our kind."

The clapping of leaves will express their mute joy,
    So airily waving in ease,

And from the dense forests, oh, "Love-bound,"
　"Love-bound,"
Comes floating along on the breeze.

The stars in their courses, the waves of the sea,
　All join in the chorus, Love-bound.
Sweet lily-bells scatter their perfume afar,
　And pansies the glad notes resound.

The child's merry laughter's a ripple of glee;
　A necklace of pearls are its tears,
As Love-bound through all the sweet joys of its life
　And Love-bound through all of its fears.

The unwritten music of Nature in song
　A love-note for lovers to hear,
So sweetly it sings from the heart to the heart,
　"If Love-bound, you 've nothing to fear."

But treasured for aye in the depths of the soul,
  A great wealth of love.   We agree,
More strong bound are they, who most truly are
  free.
My Lover, I'm Love-bound to thee.

OAKLAND, 1875.

TO MY LOVE.

May 3d, 1874.

MY love loves me, and I love him;
    Our lives in unison we trim,
To joy or sorrow, weal or woe,
As onward through life's path we go.

We note the birthdays, not aghast;
Each finds us older than the last
Only in name: our hearts keep young;
The notes of age we leave unsung.

Count not the years, so swift they fly,
They drop, as withered leaves, to die;
Their purpose having served for all,
'T were well they like the leaves should fall;

But by our love to count the years,
Much stronger, then, life's work appears;
By higher aims, expanding thought,
And deeds not in our own strength wrought.

Ah! tell me not you 're forty-four;
Across the threshold, through the door,
I see thy youth in manhood's hour,
Crowning thy life with greater power.

Still keener grows the mind with years;
Thy soul no question asks of fears;
The vision, with its longer range,
Will grasp still greater truths and strange.

Then tell me not you 're forty-four,
For I will know almost a score
Of years has borne us on the wing,
Since first our plighted troth did sing.

THE OFFICE.

WITHIN your office walls,
    A nameless rest, of quiet and repose,
Broods like a spirit great.
A living, loving, human tenderness,
    Within your breast finds vent,
And wafts its fragrance, on the air you breathe,
    To all humanity,
And thus distils a sweeter perfume's dawn,
    Than upturned violets,
Kissed daily with the dews of early morn.

LOVE'S DREAM.

OH, give me your dream, Love,
   Your love dream of me,
With thought drifting far
   To my home by the sea,
As, wrapt in the arms of the night,
   You feel on your cheek
The sweet breath of a rose,
   Entwining your heart
   In its soft velvet close ;
Believing you 're roaming the wide world with me,
Are roaming the wide world with me.

LOVE'S DREAM.

Oh, give me your dream, Love;
   A vision it grows
To charming white lilies,
   So unlike the rose.
Look into their beautiful depths,
   For over your senses
A fragrance is thrown,
   Surpassing the perfume
   Of flowers unknown,
Enfolding your heart in its fancies so free,
Your heart in its fancies so free.

But in the gray dawning,
   As o'er you may hover
The phantom-like presence
   Of me, your "One-Lover,"
The rustling of nature's wakening
   Will scatter the shadowy
   Forms of your dreams,

Possessing the spirit
In raptures supreme,
Like some unseen things, they will fly on their wings,
Away they will fly on their wings.

O'er crag and o'er hillside,
And far down the glen
Through thicket and forest,
Through river and fen,
You come to a beautiful lake :
You dream it is fleeing ;
To catch it you spring,
Swift as antelopes fly
Too late, too late — it wings.
You are awake, and no more of joy will it bring,
Ay, no more of joy will it bring.

BONDAGE.

There are great degrees of bondage
   Caused by life's surging tide;
Very many are the fancies
   Which in the soul abide,
And yield a subtle influence
   That love is sure to gain
Sooner or later o'er the hearts
   Of all mankind in twain.
For Cupid hurls his fiery darts,
   And dances with delight
At the sure havoc that attends
   His arrows in their flight.
Up to some lonely cabin door
   On mountain side he rides,
From his quiver draws his arrow,
   From bow it quickly glides.

Bound hand and foot the maiden cries,
Nor knows from whence her thraldom comes.
She feels the magnet in his eyes,
She fears the force that from him flies,
And yet she yields in sweet dismay
Her own sweet will to his own way.

Each moment as a flash of light,
Each fleeting hour a twinkling star,
Kindling for aye life's darkest night
With all that's good if used aright;
Crowning the future of her life
With all that's precious to a wife.

Oh, how sweet the wifely pledge of love!
   How holy! how divine!
As it draws its nature from above,
   It will both hearts entwine.
But to love, and then to part! Well nigh
   The fountains of the heart

Will burst in twain, as friends must die,
   And from our lives depart.
From such deep grief while here we dwell,
   Oh, is there no surcease?
And must our hearts with sorrow swell,
   Till death shall bring release?

COUNT THE WEEKS BY SUNDAYS.

COUNT not the days of absence,
    As they go dragging on,
So wearily the moments pass,
    When those we love are gone.

But count the time by Sundays,
    More swiftly will it fly;
Of all the many weeks from home,
~~Four~~ *Three* Sabbaths have gone by.

Count not the days of absence,
    One day — one day agone;
Count by the fleeting Sabbaths :
    A week will then have flown.

*T*HERE are murmuring brooks,
    Traversing life through shady nooks,
Where never a ray of the sun peers through,
To gladden the sound with its cheerful hue.
There are gladsome rivulets scattered round,
Kissing and washing the pebbly ground,
Over which they flow with such merry glee,
Thoughts of grief from the listeners flee.

SUNSHINE ON THE CHAMBER CEILING.

CREEPING into our houses,
  Through the window-pane,
Slanting through the blinds ajar,
  Sunlight gleams again.

Sparkling in its liquid light,
  In flows the morning,
Filling full our sleeping-rooms
  With the gay dawning.

Watch the rays so swift they glide,
  With their stencil train,
Tracing, with an artist's hand,
  Pictures that enchain.

Now they're sketching maple boughs,
    Swaying to and fro;
Out and in, among the trees,
    Birds are singing low.

Look! our neighbor's chimney-top,
    One can there define,
Quite an ancient castle tower,
    From the sunny Rhine.

Onward, through the Gothic blinds,
    Comes a vessel sailing,
Prow and stern and mizzen-mast
    Frescoing the ceiling.

See the proudly sailing craft;
    Swings the sun around;
One can see the billows heave,
    With her every bound.

Look! a cloud is passing now;
   Watch it rise and fall,
O'er our pretty landscape fair,
   Like a sable pall.

Pictures of the sunshine,
   You have chased our dreams
From off our sleepy couches,
   By your golden beams.

SUMMER CLOUDS.

SOFT fleecy clouds dot the sky here and there,
    Tripping like fairies, through the summer air;
Swiftly they move across the azure blue,
Piling o'er each other, floating in dew.

Oh, ye snowy mountain peaks, drifting high,
Castellated pictures making in the sky,
Whence do you come, and whither do you go?
Tell me, snowy, fleecy clouds, floating low?

SNOW-FLAKES.

OH, watch the tiny snow-flakes,
    Falling, falling thro' the air,
The many million snow-flakes,
    With upturned faces fair.

How they jostle one another,
    Career and tumble all around,
O'er and o'er each other falling,
    Till they cover all the ground.

See the children's happy faces,
    Pressed against the window-pane,
Listening to the muffled music
    Of the snow-flakes in the lane.

Higher, higher, frozen raindrops,
    Spreading out in feathery foam,
Piles a fairy, glistening blanket
    Over all so close and warm.

But we older ones are thinking,
    Of the million stifling cares,
Falling, falling all around us,
    Constant burden of our prayers.

How they jostle one another,
    To and fro the whole day long,
O'er and o'er each other tumbling,
    Till we know not right from wrong;

Till our hearts grow weary, weary,
    And the living, working brain,
Bending 'neath the growing burden,
    Shrinks from life's unrest in vain.

But, as 'neath the piling snow-flakes,
    Every germ of Nature lies
Dormant, restful, till the Springtime
    Calls it gladly to arise;

So the soul in heavenly pureness,
    From the cares of life shall come,
Singing songs of resurrection,
    Winging upward to its home.

June 23, 1876.

THE SONG OF THE OCEAN.

THE song of the ocean is merry or sad,
    As hearts of its hearers are weary or glad;
But all the night through and for all the day long
It breathes the same cadence, it sings the same song.

   " Roll on, my dusky waves, roll on,
     And break your crests yon shore upon;
    Your mates shall follow in your wake.
    Roll on, my dusky waves, and break."

To children, it's sweet as the songs of the dove;
To maiden, it is always singing of love;
To manhood, whose spirit is full of desire,
The ocean has power his soul to inspire.

THE SONG OF THE OCEAN.

> *" Roll on, my dusky waves, roll on,*
> *And break your crests yon shore upon ;*
> *Your mates shall follow in your wake.*
> *Roll on, my dusky waves, and break."*

The song of the ocean is more importune,
When storm winds are howling their deep notes in June,
When lightnings flash bright, and the loud thunder raves,
And great waters surge from their innermost caves.

> *" Roll on, my dusky waves, roll on,*
> *And break your crests yon shore upon ;*
> *Your mates shall follow in your wake.*
> *Roll on, my dusky waves, and break."*

The waves that are raging, no longer will take
To far-distant beaches their white caps to break,

But high over mountains of billowy foam,
Away in mid-ocean, they 'll dash to their home.

" Roll on, my dusky waves, roll on,
And break your crests yon shore upon ;
Your mates shall follow in your wake.
Roll on, my dusky waves, and break."

The song of the ocean is full of despair ;
Deep moanings it utters upon the night air, —
Such moanings, oh, what are the thoughts that they stir,
What depths do they rouse, in my soul's lethargy !

" Roll on, my dusky waves, roll on,
And break your crests yon shore upon ;
Your mates shall follow in your wake.
Roll on, my dusky waves, and break."

Like yonder waves dashing, they rush o'er my brain,
And fill me with courage their truth to attain ;

They roll back the trammels from off of the soul;
The spirit grows stronger its life to control.

> *Then thought surge on, forever surge,*
> *The heart from all of evil purge,*
> *As pure and white as ocean shore*
> *Is washed by waves forevermore.*

TO H. H.'S QUESTION, "WHICH WAY WENT SUMMER?"

L IST ! the voice of the Red-Rose:
"These flowers must decay,
For north winds are blowing
  Their petals away;
But warm is my heart in the
  Cherishing ground,
And summer is with me, far
  Under the mound.
Again to your world we will
  Come by and by;
New roses will bloom to me,
  Death to belie.
Oh, life of my life, and sweet
  Breath of my breath,

Together we flee winter's
 Semblance of death."

But what saith the Honey-Bee:
 " Frozen? Nay! nay!
In cosey cells dormant with
 Summer I stay;
Together we're nestling the
 Whole winter through,
Renewing our strength and our
 Beauty for you,
Where violets, mayflowers, and
 Even the clover,
In sweet-scented perfumes, all
 Over us hover.
We're resting and dreaming
 Of gladness, of spring,
When, friend, to your world again
 Summer we'll bring."

And nestled beneath the soft
    Wings of the Bird,
The chirpings of summer
    May always be heard:
"Though winter shall drive us
    Afar from the north,
She cannot compel us to
    Stifle our mirth;
But sweeter than ever the
    Songs and the flowers
When the birds and the summer
    Return to these bowers."
Thus answered the Song-Bird,
    The Blossom, the Bee,
"I keep the bright summer
    Forever with me."

THE ENGADINE VILLAGES.

THE Engadine! Beautiful Engadine!
   Many of Switzerland's most treasured peaks,
  Standing around thy villages, still keep
A watch over thy lakes and river Inn;
Their lofty heads, covered with snow, are seen
   Glistening in sunlight, or in clouds asleep;
   And, like a Gordian knot tied fast, bespeak
The full protection of their stately mien.

Piz-Languard, monarch of the chain, a seer:
"Oh, Engadine, nothing shall enter here
   To mar the beauty of thy hidden grace;
These mountain homes, to us so very dear,
These homes of honest folk of sturdy race,
Most tenderly we hold in strong embrace."

SMOKE OF THE CITY.

Have you ever watched a city,
    In the early morn,
And seen the smoke go circling up
    To catch the early dawn?

Higher, higher, watched it rising,
    Floating to the skies,
Lost in yonder atmosphere, go
    From your wondering eyes?

Have you listened for the carols,
    Song-birds flying there,
Thought within those vapory clouds
    Are angels' dwellings fair?

Looked on palace, mill, and hamlet,
    Watched it rise and fall,
Till wakened from your revery
    By the breakfast call?

Then you do not know the pleasure
    Of chambers in your house,
Which overlook the city homes
    From windows east and south.

THE THUNDER.

OH, hark! in the distance
    Comes crashing and rumbling
  The thunder;
It bids me take warning.
You are not in earnest,
    Artillery?
For see, the bright sunshine
Belies your prediction
    Of rain.
But still you are talking;
Your roaring around me,
    Oh, thunder,
Disturbs meditation,
And bids me take warning.

AUTUMN.

MY chamber resembles
　　Arcadian bowers,
With its long trailing vines
　　And autumnal flowers.
But the bright glowing coals,
　　In the blackened grate,
Are laughing at beauty
　　For blooming so late.

NOVEMBER.

HIE thee, bleak and dull November!
    Thou art too rude for song;
Such piercing wails of wind and rain
    Create a sense of wrong.

For song of birds I list in vain,
    For humming of the bee;
Instead, thou moanest piteously,
    Afar o'er land and sea.

As wilder blows the north wind's wrath,
    The little laughing rill
Gives up its ripple to the frost,
    And lies so cold and still.

Rivers are wrapped in winding-sheets,
    The lakes are frozen fast,
When deeper grow thy mutterings,
    When wilder blows the blast.

Thus Mother Earth reluctant yields
    Her heart to thy embrace,
And daily sees the life depart
    Of beauty from her face.

So hie thee, chill November, hie!
    Away with clouds and rain!
Give us the sparkling feath'ry flakes,
    Of cold December's reign,

To shield the tender germs of earth
    From all the winds that blow,
While bringing us the pleasures, rare,
    Born of the drifting snow.

TO-MORROW.

There is no to-morrow;
   Like a phantom it flies,
On the wings of the morning,
   From our longing eyes.

For the gray dawn is stealing,
   While in slumber we rest,
And to-day smiles upon us;
   It endeth our quest.

PICTURES.

A DARK, sequestered vale,
Where whippoorwills, and larks, and
robins gay
Play hide-go-seek whene'er the branches sway;
Music of little brooks, trickling anew
Through latticed fern leaves, wet with morning dew.

Bright visions to the eye,
Of green fields, waving with the summer grain;
Of herds, now lowing in the meadow lane.
Far off the gently flowing river winds,
As here and there its level bed it finds.

A sandy, rolling beach
Basks in the sunshine when old Ocean sleeps,
Then when the tide comes creeping from the deeps.

Unlike the rushing tides of life, we find
A dreamy listlessness steals o'er the mind.

A pebbly, glistening beach,
Washed by the surging, mighty, roaring waves,
Breaking their snowy crests, as o'er it raves
The foaming cataract of the stormy sea,
Lashed by the furious winds from o'er the lea.

A cloudy, threatening sky;
The thunders roar and through the valleys crash,
Echoing afar: — the lightning's vivid flash
Reveals the sky, leaden with rain and mist,
Flooding mountain heights with lights of amethyst.

Bold, rocky cliffs stand forth,
Their sides adorned with hemlock, spruce, and vine,
Waving their topmost boughs, to rhythmic line
Of plunging waterfalls, anear their feet:
Thus do the wildest scenes in nature meet.

THE OCEAN'S LULLABY.

Rock me
    To sleep, waves,
  And over me roll
The tenderest music from out of your soul.
    Rock me
    To sleep, waves,
  And over me keep
The strictest of vigils, the while that I sleep.

    Keep me
    Asleep, waves,
  While nature shall rest
This brain that is weary upon your great breast.

Keep me

Asleep, waves,

And over me weep

The tears of your raindrops, at times while I sleep.

Wake me

From sleep, waves,

And let my soul hear

The song of the ocean when storm-clouds appear.

Wake me

From sleep, waves ;

Its music will keep

My heart full of courage, life's harvest to reap.

SQUIBNOCKET.

SUNRISE ON LAKE SUPERIOR.

THE rosy tints that lie along
    The eastern shore at break of dawn
Are brighter than the maiden's blush,
And deeper than the evening's flush.

A moment, and they mount, they fly
Across the azure of the sky,
Dispersing from the night the shades.
Glorious light the earth pervades,

With songs of welcome, from the lips
Of roses red, from lily tips;
From insects, beasts, and birds that sing,
To make the morning welkin ring;

From rolling, rippling, sparkling waves,
As sunshine with its glory laves;
From glistening shafts of pearly beams,
Piercing beneath the mountain streams.

All human voices, tuned to praise,
Should listen to this call, and raise
Their heartfelt thanks to make replete
The welcome to the day complete.

Oh, rich indeed the sun's foresight,
To herald thus the day aright,
Waking to life the heart of earth,
Making each morning a new birth.

STEAMER PEERLESS, *Aug.* 13, 1872.

THE NIGHT WINDS.

THE night winds!
　　What are they saying,
Twisting the branches from off the trees,
　　Knocking the bricks
　　From the chimneys?
Will their voices let nothing appease?

　　Not the same sweet
　　Tale they are telling;
It depends on the listener's ear:
　　To some wailing
　　And dire destruction;
But to others they breathe of good cheer.

Some, in dreaming,
Think they are zephyrs,
Sighing so sweetly, floating in air;
Some feel the tread
Of the Storm King,
As he marches from out of his lair.

Listen, as he
Gathers his forces,
And encircles some poor stricken sail;
Over the waves
Tossing his victim,
When caught in a "midsummer-night's" gale.

Thus to travel
With eager swiftness,
To be borne on the wings of the wind,
What freedom,
What wonder, delight,
Oh, what pleasure we mortals could find!

Comes the morning,
Night winds are dying
And decreasing as shades fly away;
Round the corners,
Soft winds whispering,
A good-morning to all, and good-day.

STORM IN CALIFORNIA.

1875.

So wild the storm to-night!
    Whence comes such unutterable grief?
Borne on the breath of this
Tempestuous sea of wind and rain,
A spirit's moaning piteously.
A passionate gush of weeping
Comes against the window-pane;
Then a louder, wilder wailing
Is heard above the gale.
Whence comest thou? O spirit,
What is thy thought to night?
Tell us thy purpose and thy aim;
Why weepest thou against the pane?

Against the earth, and sea, and air,
Against our hearts, so full of care,
Against all laughter, joy, and mirth,
To which thy happier hours gave birth,
Are thy tears so unavailing?
Hast thou no power to save
The sinking ones upon the deep?
No power to help the struggling
Or suffering ones of earth?
No power to shield the homeless waif,
Nor protection to vouchsafe?
Whence comest thou? Oh, spirit,
Wild, wild, thy voice to-night;
Whence comest thou? Oh, tell us,
Or we perish by thy might!
But the darkness gathered blackness,
At the moaning and the crying
Of the raging storm.
Our minds were filled with terror,

At the wild winds' deep implore;
We shuddered as we listened,
And the rattling casements drear
Filled our hearts with inward fear,
When nearer came a furious blast,
Of the tempest rushing past.

. . . .

A lull! we feel our hearts cease beating:
    In the stillness;
We hear the eucalyptus-trees
Shaking out their willow leaves;
And in the distance, sobbing, sobbing out its pain,
Wings the storm departing,
With its trailing garments, heavy with the rain,
Weighted with the burden of its prayers,
The ceaseless, moaning burden of its prayers.

COMING SNOW-STORM.

THE day is dull; the air is chill;
    A leaden hue o'ershadows the sill
Of the great blue dome we call the sky,
And veils the bright sunshine from our eye.

The morning wanes; a feathery flake
Comes floating from the darkening lake,
That hangs overhead; its waters bear
Rare liquid gems, in the freezing air.

Faster, faster the snow-flakes fall;
The air is gay as a fairies' ball.
Come one, come all, a numberless throng,
Now dancing, waltzing, skipping along.

Flake follows flake with merry glee,
Rousing the notes of chick-a-dee-dee;
Jostling each other in swift descent,
The force of the storm is soon o'erspent.

So beautiful the world to-night
Enfolded warm in her ermine white;
So quiet lies the new-fallen snow
Over the face of the earth below.

SEA-SHELLS.

BEAUTIFUL shells, whisper to me, from the depths
    Of the deep blue sea;
The sweet stories of old, which fairies have told,
    Oh, tell them to me!
Pearl nautilus shell, with your two dainty sails,
    And floating so true,
Your bark is so frail, will it weather the gales,
    With its tiny crew?

And you, rainbow shells, which for ages have slept
    In deep hidden caves,
Save when on curious errands bent, you've crept
    Above the dark waves;
Pretty snails, measuring your length among the reeds
    Along the far shore,

Oh, what can you tell, of the old Ocean's deeds,
    Of interest more?

For daintiest texture and beauty of mould,
    Can nothing compare
That's grown in the depths of the ocean's fold
    With corals, so fair.
Oh, tell of your strange weird life, ye tiny shells,
    How surely you grow
Into flowers and endless forms, from living cells,
    By the waves' overflow.

OHO! YE WINDS.

OHO! ye winds, from out your hidden caves,
    What list ye? what the story you would tell?
  How, o'er the foaming sea, you 've thrown a spell,
And tossed high over rocks the stormy waves?
With ceaseless energy their surface raves,
    Until the voices of the deep, a knell
    Forever sounding on their courses, quell
The murm'rings of the sea, in watery graves.

Oho! ye winds, these are the thoughts ye bring:
    Our purpose strong, whate'er our work to do;
Though ghosts of deeds forgot, forever ring
    Their strains into our ears, we will not rue
The past, but onward press, with courage sing,
    Our will is strong our life's work well to do.

SQUIBNOCKET.

A FRAIL bark loosed from its moorings
    Floated out on the river of time;
Freighted with human life, she bore
    This precious child of mine.

MOTHERHOOD.

BABY is coming!
 The young mother's days
Overflow with a world of delight;
 For baby is coming!
 A bit of self coming!
 From whence? and for what?
 The strange, the new thought,
Takes hold of the young mother's heart.

 But coming from whence?
 This breath of new life,
That is stirring my being to-night;
 Tell me, coming from whence?

Sweetest spirit, from whence
Do you come, changing
The whole of my life
To motherhood, born of the wife?

For what? do you know
For what, baby mine?
Vital germ, clinging close to my heart,
Only this do *I* know,
Only this *can I* know,
There comes to my life
New purpose to hold
More sacred the truths of my soul.

For my baby's coming,
My own baby's coming,
Spark divine, to this bosom of mine.
O Saviour! such longing!

List, list to my longing,
To bear and to rear,
For Thee, Lord, for Thee,
This life Thou hast trusted to me.

THE FIRST BABY.

ONLY a wee little bundle in white;
　　Only a baby-boy born in the night;
Only a lover and husband?　Ay, more,
Proudly a father now paces the floor.

Closely a dear mother nestles beside,
Cooing to cunningest baby alive,
Strangely to realize hopes that at morn,
Merely seemed fancies, ere baby was born.

Gazing in silence, the father's heart thrills;
This life from his life, new purpose instils:
Softly the mother caresses the face;
Together they pray for wisdom and grace.

"Father in Heaven, Thy presence we crave;
Watch o'er his pathway from cradle to grave;
Thy left arm to save, Thy right hand to guide,
Cherishing Love, do Thou always abide."

1889.

HELEN.

God knows best. I wrote a few verses on the death of the beautiful Helen, the evening her tiny feet first walked the golden streets, but failed to express the rare vision of light, the beauty of her who had dwelt among us, so like a spirit. It cannot be told; one must have seen Helen, looked into the depths of her beautiful pensive eyes, touched her fairy form, to realize what it must be to be an angel.

"Helen, Helen, pet, where are you?"
   On the evening breeze so clear.
"I am here," sweet Helen answered;
   "Here am I, my mamma dear."

"Come, my Helen dear, I want you."
   "I don't want to; must I, why?
I am playing with the squirrels;
   I'll come, mamma, by and by."

"Helen, Helen, oh, where are you?"
  Breaking hearts are calling here;
But the same pure spirit answers,
  "I am near you, mamma dear."

"Come, our Helen dear, we want you."
  Tender is the sweet reply:
"I am happy now with Jesus;
  You'll come, mamma, by and by."

*So happy are days in the springtime of life,
   The glad budding springtime of youth,
When no thought of the morrow, full of cares,
   Steals away the sweet promise of truth.*

CHILDHOOD PASSING.

PAST, all past is sunny childhood,
    Like a swiftly flowing stream,
When the heart is full of sunshine,
    When all life is like a dream.

When the slightest wish is welcomed,
    Mother's kiss each sorrow healed,
Then the birthdays were like mile-stones,
    Standing out upon life's field.

One by one from out life's quiver,
    Years are plucked beyond your power;
Youth is fleeing faster from you
    Than your childhood's sunny hour.

Youth, with all its richer treasure,
    Gathered from life's hidden springs,
One cannot begin to fathom,
    All the wealth of soul it brings.

Do not, though so often worried
    By the thinking, working brain,
Lose the trusting faith of childhood,
    Lose what cannot come again.

INTO YOUTH.

MY daughter, the gray day is breaking;
    Among the tree-tops thrills the dawning
Of the coming of the morning,
    Of thy youth.

Mark it in thy shadow, longer grown,
Longings of the heart, thou wilt not own,
Springing from seed in childhood sown;
    It is youth.

Full fifteen years have fled before thee,
Joyous years from many cares so free,
Happy years so full of merry glee,
    Pass into youth!

Do not backward turn the wheels of time,
Nor, fairest maid, these thoughts of thine;
Press onward to life's highest prime,
    Through thy youth.

Never fear thy greatest deeds to dare;
The deepest truths thy thoughts will share,
If spoken the most earnest prayer
    Of thy youth.

No feverish heat of noonday's sun
Will bring the goal for which you run,
Unless life's work has been well done
    In early youth.

For in the morning's calmer hour,
When sweet repose lends greater power
To all thy work, great is the dower
    Of well-lived youth.

"TO A YOUNG CHILD."

Translated from Victor Hugo.

OH, child! in thy beautiful infancy,
    Do not envy our riper years
When the heart, oft enslaved, is rebellious,
    And our laughter more sad than your tears.

Your days, at once careless and sweet, you forget;
    They all pass as a breath on the air,
As a voice full of joy, like the Halcyon's,
    Vanishing over the sea so rare.

Rejoice in the morning, joy in the springing
    Of childhood; its hours are the flowers.
Strip not their petals more quickly than time;
    Wreathe the one to the other's fair hours.

"TO A YOUNG CHILD."

The years let them come, that destiny appoints you;
    The regrets and false friendships unkind,
Those faults without hope, which pride disavows,
    And those pleasures which sadden the mind.

But laugh while you may, ignore destiny's sway,
    Do not sadden your brow full of grace;
Your eye full of azure, child's mirror of peace,
    Will reflect heaven's soul in your face.

"COUNT LIFE BY DEEDS."

GO, thou fair soul, and be at rest,
    We would not bid thee stay, though hearts must break.
We would not longer keep thee here in life's
Great press of earnest toil, to struggle on.
No life is ended, till, for good or ill,
The work that's given it to do is finished.
And with thy life's great end so well attained,
We would not bid thee stay, though greater seems
Our loss, and harder still to bear, each day
As time goes on, and months and years go by,
Without thy daily presence here to bide.
Thou hast not died so young as many men,
Whose burdens fall, at threescore years and ten.

"COUNT LIFE BY DEEDS."

We count not life by " figures on a dial,"
" But by deeds ; " and every moment of thy
Well-spent life, thy strong and vigorous youth,
Was as a ling'ring year in some men's lives.

FRIENDSHIP.

IS friendship, with you, a
    "Midsummer night's dream,"
That the first breath of winter
Leaves to wither?
Then wait ere thou pluck
The dead flower from the stalk,
And ask in the silence,
Wherein lies the fault
Of this fresh young love,
Thus to wither?

REVERIES.

DREAMILY, in the chambers of the heart,
    The fancies, which each life possesses, dwell;
Oft will the bidding of our thoughts compel
The memories that beckon, and hopes that start
The pulses coursing, to at once depart.
    For, there is another being, a kell,
    Living so keen within the soul, a spell
Is wrought upon the mind, its counterpart.
My soul! sometime this dual nature twain
    Will burst the bands asunder and be free,
Will recognize new powers of life to gain,
    Will give new force, that all our senses be
More keenly strung to Nature's sweetest strain,
    And we at one will be with our feoffee.

SQUIBNOCKET, *August*, 1894.

SAVED.

SHE tore the roses from her hair;
    She dashed the pale pinks 'neath her feet;
  She cried, " And I will stem the tide,
The earth will roam, and cross the sea,
But I will know that I am free.
What care I for a world of scorn?
What care I for its pomp and show?
I will have flowers that I love best,
And hide their sweetness in my breast."

But no one knew how great the pain
With which her spirit prayed again,
"Oh, come, my mother, back," she cried,
" From your bright home beyond the tide,

To put your arms about my neck ;
Thus can your love my troubles check.
You know what life is here and there ;
You know what human life can bear,
And knowing, can my spirit save,
To live life's mystery to the grave."

A maid both brave and strong was she,
For in God's grace her soul was free,
Though born to drink life's bitterest lees,
Be tossed for aye on roughest seas ;
As storms beset her own frail bark,
They seem her purposes to mock,
But naught can move her from that rock,
By which she learns what life attains,
When in God's love the soul remains.

We know not, mortals ne'er may know
Until temptation's power assails,

What grace from hidden streams can flow,
What wondrous love from God will glow,
When, in the soul's most direful needs,
It for infinite wisdom pleads,
And finds in faith such perfect strength
As on God's word to rest at length;
Such trusting makes the spirit pure,
And proves life's purposes secure.

REMEMBRANCE.

THE flowers are beautiful, my friend ;
    Love no sweeter gift could send,
A breath of friendship's living spring
From affection's depths they bring.

Blue violets, with modest grace,
Look me kindly in the face ;
And heliotrope, with fragrance rare,
Sweetly scents the evening air.

The orange blossom's perfumed kiss
Greets the senses, — fills with bliss ;
To waiting spirits, glad surprise,
Heaven's perfume from the skies.

The calla lifts its cup of white
Heavenward for a drink of light;
The morning drops a tear of dew
In its depths of pearly hue.

The rosebud, sweeter than the rest,
Every leaf from heart to crest,
Is like the folding of great love,
Round about us from above.

Anon the bud's unfolding leaves
Give their fragrance to the breeze;
So will the cares our lives possess,
Yield themselves to Christ's caress;

New courage to life's work impart,
Greater longings to the heart,
A perfume which no flower can give, —
'T is immortality to live.

DREAMS.

WE weigh not the truth in our dreams;
    We think not of time, nor of space.
Our loved ones are with us again:
    We dwell in a moment of grace,

So real, so blissful, so true,
    We seem to ourselves wide-awake;
No thought, in a moment or two,
    The spell, the illusion, will break;

Though ofttimes before we have known
    How fleeting the joys of a dream;
When sleep from our eyelids has flown,
    No longer are things as they seem.

A FRAGMENT.

THERE are some things we oft confess,
    The which we do not now possess;
But once could they increase our store,
We would not ask for one thing more.

O vain delusion! vain desires!
To have, will but increase the fires
Which burn within each human breast;
It is the human soul's unrest.

*NOBLEST deeds are only wrought
    From out the realm of noble thought;
Man's aspirations are as naught,
Unless such inspiration's sought.*

1776–1876.

FIRM amidst the rigging of a
   Miniature "Ship of State,"
That, in its youthful vigor grown,
   First felt its future great,
Stood the "Immortal Washington,"
   With one hand at the helm,
Steering, through seas of blood and woe,
   To anchorage, a realm.

His stalwart form, commanding those
   Less hopeful in the fight,
Inspired all hearts with courage firm
   To battle for the right,
Until their arms victorious
   Proclaimed with loud huzzas

A nation born to march for aye
    Beneath the "Stripes and Stars."

Since then a century has flown;
    This stalwart "Ship of State"
Has stood the strain of battles fierce,
    Of civil war's debate,
That shook her rafters, beam to end,
    Plunged her in deepest flood;
'T was then the immortal Lincoln steered
    The ship through seas of blood.

But now, ye clarion voices, ring!
    From hamlet, hill, and town,
From broad expanse of prairie land,
    From Rocky Mountain crown;
To proclaim a nation's birthday;
    One hundred years have flown,
Since, in the throes of freedom's war,
    America was born.

Let the booming of the cannon,
    Once heard at Bunker Hill,
Re-echo all the country round,
    Our souls with rapture thrill.
So great has been the progress made,
    So great our nation's fame,
How glorious, we can but sing,
    Our nation's great acclaim.

Let not fierce hand of party rule
    Her stalwart sinews shake,
Nor fiercer hands of anarchy
    Her highest courage break.
Let not man's fierce ambitions prove,
    For wealth's unseemly gain,
A greater curse to rule the land,
    Our nation's glory stain.

JAMES A. GARFIELD.

GARFIELD lies slain !
   The bulwark of the nation's Ship of
      State
Creaks as it rides the stormy sea of death :
Around the world is heard the pistol-shot,
   Garfield lies slain !
Then all is still — and silence,
A dread and awful silence, now prevails ;
Millions of people wait with anxious
Hearts' bated breath the next electric flash :
   He lives ! he lives !
Our nation's chosen leader, still he lives ;
The news to all the world fresh courage gives.
   He lives ! he lives !

"Thank God, he lives!"
Comes flashing o'er the wires from far and near;
And joining hearts and hands, the nation, true
To its great destiny, marches boldly on,
 Though Garfield lies
'Twixt life on earth and hence for eighty days.
The Ship of State upon her shoulders bore,
Through all those anxious weeks of her baptism,
The treasured life; cradled upon her breast
 The martyred President;
Most hopeful that the nation's full reunion
Might come through another benediction
 Of sacrifice!

 Such crucial days!
Upward and onward, to a higher plane,
Moved the wide world, to which the sacrifice
Had suddenly uplifted all mankind;
 So great the cost!

Garfield, by long suffering, drew the pulses of
The world to beat as one against such crime.
But must the cup be drained to bitter dregs?
No power on earth the fatal blow can stay.

  The nation took the cup,
And drank, as only they can drink, who know
That from such potions comes a better day.

  Right must prevail!

NUREMBERG'S GABLES.

1885.

OLD Nuremberg!
  Poets have sung thy wondrous
    gables from
Days mediæval, and now they tune my lyre
To tell thee of their beauty once again.
  Like entering wedge, those many-storied
Roofs above the eaves, sharp-ridged, pierce
    To yonder sky.

  Old Nuremberg!
No merely simple words can paint in rhyme,
  The pictures which, against the evening sky,
Thy pointed spires and gabled roofs can make;
  For who can tell where homes and churches end,
Or clouds begin, as cometh down the night
    O'er ancient town.

Old Nuremberg!
Methinks to climb upon thy terraced roofs,
  And lay my weary head among the clouds
That nestle there so closely round thy brow,
  Would fill my spirit full of inward peace,
And bring some revelation of the power
    That dwells in Art!

Old Nuremberg!
Thou didst inspire our Albrecht Dürer's soul.
  The same thou wroughtst through Master Workman
    Kraft, —
Who sought with tireless energy and force
  The soul of beauty there to trace anew,
In carved woodwork and in chiselled stone,
    In cathedral walls.

Old Nuremberg!
I think of all the ages that have sped
  Since first thy gabled roofs, cathedral spires,

And dormer windows (sleepy eyes, half closed)
    Have caught the sunshine and the balmy air,
The storms of winter, and the lightning's glare,
        From yonder skies!

        Old Nuremberg!
Thou hast ever sought to bring to human souls,
    Living beneath thy roofs, some knowledge fair,
Of life beyond the deep blue of thy skies;
    That life which many poets taught and sung,
That sculptors wrought and artists daily sought
        Within thy walls.

        Old Nuremberg!
What is it dulls the chisel, holds the thought,
    This living thought within the human brain?
Did I say life beyond? Forgive my words:
    The life that now is, claims our constant work,
Demands the soul within to wake and live,
        And of its courage give.

THE REV. JOSEPH HAVEN, D. D.

SORROWING, yet rejoicing!
    Who can reveal
The wealth of love, the grief we feel,
When such as he have lived and died.
Have walked the earth, then crossed the tide,
And we, though weeping, must press on
Through all life's busy, jostling throng,
Until our own life's journey's done.

Sorrowing is not mourning,
    For Jesus wept!
His soul was stirred when Lazarus slept
The sleep of death, and he did weep:
Sweet tears of consolation given,
To comfort; when our hearts are riven,

His tears assure us 't is not wrong
For us to weep when friends are gone.

Sorrowing, yet rejoicing!
    We will rejoice.
For such a life gives ample proof,
That all the filling of the woof
We weave in life is full of joy;
For sorrow is but Christ's alloy
With joy, to give the light and shade
To human life, which will not fade.

Sorrowing, yet rejoicing!
    He bids us live.
Well might the glance the angels give,
Be always pitying, for the need
Is great to comfort on our way.
And thus a blessing day by day
Comes wafted from the other shore,
From out this life that's gone before.

TO WHITTIER,

ON THE ANNIVERSARY OF HIS SEVENTIETH BIRTHDAY.

As sunlight on the mountain-top,
    As moonlight on the sea,
Most brilliantly the lapse of years
    Wafts back its light to thee.

Full-orbed, thy sympathetic soul,
    For all the rights of men,
Did struggle valiantly and long,
    By word and deed and pen,

Until the conflict waxed to war,
    And slavery was slain, —
That blackest woe of human might,
    Scourging our nation's name.

How looks the battlefield of life,
   How stirs thy soul within,
As rising to the snowy peaks
   Of threescore years and ten?

What visions from a land of rest
   Float o'er thy peaceful brow?
What memories of all the past
   Are ever present now?

Most sacredly the ministry
   Of many a ripened year
Shall crown thy brow with honor,
   Thou blessed prophet seer.

FAIR DRYBURGH ABBEY.

FAIR Dryburgh Abbey! Tell me!
From whence art thou?
And whither dost thou go?
A thought within the brain of man
For centuries has stood embalmed.
Thy ivy-covered walls, fast falling to decay,
Are full of life, so much of thought is still expressed
In what remains
Of shafts and casings,
Nave and transept,
Choir and cross,
In chapters crowning fluted columns bold,

That it were well
To see thee oft,
Though now thou stand'st in tumbled ruins old,
Upon the land.

Fair Dryburgh Abbey! Heed me!
Thy arched doorways
Are poetry of form,
So finely carved thy blocks of stone;
While balanced, as by magic,
In all its wondrous beauty, supreme o'er all,
Yonder harp window hangs amidst its wall,
And from that height,
The light of heaven,
Greatest boon to life,
Shines fair,
Through chiselled tracery, a silvery sheen,
A witchery o'er
Departed days,

So great its beauty rare, so unforeseen
      In days gone by.

    Fair Dryburgh Abbey! Listen!
      Thy cloistered cells,
      For centuries agone,
   Where dwelt Cistercian monks,
  Sincere enthusiasts of old,
Are now the eyrie homes of merry songsters bold;
Some finely carved cornice holds their fragile nests:
      The swallow, thrush,
      The meadow lark,
      And such of kin,
      Their matins hold,
Singing their lives away in happy song,
      That here they dwell,
      So glad and free,
Regardless of the past, lying so very long
      'Neath ruined walls.

Fair Dryburgh Abbey! It is sad!
 Forsaken is
 Thy banquet hall;
So grand when in its prime, but there
Remains, beneath thy vaulted roof,
Enough in which to trace the footsteps of the past:
Thy belfry's winding stair, now lost in air;
 Thy corridors,
 Thy columns fine;
 Deep window-seats,
 In which to dream.
Each weird spot seems dearer than the last,
 To picture scenes
 Poets have sung
Of revelries within these Abbey walls
 In days of old.

Fair Dryburgh Abbey! Listen!
 Midst crumbling stones,
 With ivy overgrown,

St. Moden's chapel stands intact,
And guards the mortal dust
Of baronets of old within its narrow cells.
St. Mary's aisle, covered with trailing vine and moss,
In these latter days,
Holds what remains,
The earthly mould
Of an immortal mind;
The soul of Walter Scott beyond the press
Of this life's toil,
Long since has passed
And winged its way, the spirit's sure egress,
To heavenly lands.

Fair Dryburgh Abbey! Hearken!
Guard well this dust,
In shadow of its home,
Buried beneath thy lingering shades,
Its earthly resting-place.

Rich memories of the living past these ruins hold,
Treasured for aye, whilst human life shall last.
   Peace to thy walls,
   So prostrate laid;
   Peace rest on pilgrims,
   Who yet may come,
To give due homage to thine honored sage.
   When Gabriel calls,
   " Give up this dust,"
Thou too wilt fly, custodian of the age,
   Released at last.

*As the flowers grow by sunshine,
   By rain and shadows too,
So the soul's great mystic progress
   Is by what it passes through.*

COURAGE BY THE WAY.

AT times, it seemeth all progress is stayed;
    Our spirits are heavy, our bodies we lade
With burdens so very grievous to bear,
We wish, but in vain, for release from all care.

Not so the Father's intent, as we know;
" Consider the lilies afield, how they grow,"
Rings down the ages, a lesson of trust,
With purity filling the souls of the just.

From out of this care no way can we see :
When once it has grown, like the great banyan-tree,
Its roots strike deeper and deeper, we find,
Each day, it engrosses so much of our mind.

I'm thinking of what the Saviour would say,
Were He to walk with us, in person, one day:
Listen, the Father is waiting to share
The heaviest burden of all of our care;

Not to the utmost of each day's full strength,
Unfitting the soul for its best work at length.
No life should be taken at all unawares;
It is but the labor of love God requires.

GOD'S WILL.

JUST to lie here, — is this all,
    Dear Father, that Thou ask'st of me to do?

Not all, My child.   Thy life beguile
With cheerfulness and courage all the while.

But, Father, I could work and pray with far
More courage, not to lie in bed all day.

Ay, true, My child! and hence My mandate,
Lie in bed the while.
Lie, until the Sun of righteousness,
Dwelling in thy heart supreme,
Shall conquer all unrest;
Shall make it seem like work,
Done in My way, not thine.

Work! like work to prostrate lie?
Let all my hopes and wishes, one by one,
For lack of power to execute, perish?
To feel the intellect grow stronger far
Than words can reach, far keener day by day,
As suffering in the body quickens life?

Suppose, My child, the lovely
Fragile flower, that's born for beauty,
Should oft complain, because no fruitage
Followed, as its beauty waned?

But, Father, cheerfully, each day to ask
That others be my feet, my hands, to bring
E'en the simplest things of life; and smother
Almost daily the many, many wants
That rise like unseen spectres in my mind,
To taunt me with my helplessness?

Just so, My child! and doing this,
To know My power is full of bliss.

Ofttimes I turn from all my body wants,
And feel Thy overflowing presence near,
Waiting to give more than my soul can ask;
Then it is that all these earthly wants subside.
So much Thy living presence means to those
Who live most truly near Thee all the while.

It were well, My child!
More quickly wilt thou know, trusting Me,
All else shall to thee added be.

Like work, indeed, it is to dwell apart
From all the world,
Within my four-walled room.
Ay, Father, that Thou know'st full well,
It is the hardest work, that yet

Thou hast given me to do.
Oh, guard me well throughout the weary days,
And free my soul at last from all the pain,
From all the struggles that this life implies,
From all the daily imperfections;
And may Thy constant love with me abide!

Full well, My child,
Thou art learning life's great lesson,
That whatsoever be thy lot,
Thou 'lt be therein content.

THE BODY'S REST.

THERE remains a rest! Ah, yes!
   Even in the midst of the great city's
Clashing noise of busy mart, and all
The heavy tread of earnest life o'erhead.
Nothing disturbs these cities of the dead,
So calm the bodies lie beneath the sod;
Nothing to mark their resting-place
But the cold gray stones,
The marble slabs, the registrar
Of the living dead — to the dead alive.

'T is well at times to think there is release
From all this toil and worrying care;
From all enticing pleasures too, as well,
That give the soul such struggles to attain.

It were well at times, I say, to realize
That some day there will come a glad release,
Else it were more than mortal life could stand
To struggle on forever.

Knowing this,
That sometime all this rush will cease,
How strong the spirit is
To live its life full purposed to the end.
For know, at any time and all, the end
Is nigh: it will not be too long delayed,
When, in some city of the dead,
Thy body too shall rest, as these now lie;
Thy spirit to the world of spirits gone,
As these have gone.

BOSTON,
"*Granary Burial Ground*,"
"1660."

UNREST.

WHEN I long for resting,
    As oft I do in pain,
In thought I'm turning ever
    To the restless sea again.

Why should the old, old ocean
    Bring thoughts of rest to me?
Because I read a lesson
    There, the Lord is teaching me.

Pain is the restless ocean,
    That's tossing to and fro;
Give way to the ceaseless motion,
    And rest you'll sooner know.

CALL FOR HELP.

HELP! for it is dark: Thy hand is not
    Leading through this lonely spot,
Else I could say, "Lord, let Thy will be done,
Until the whole of life's great battle 's won
    In Thy great name."

Help! though it is light! Dost Thou not see?
Strife is raging, wrong is rife,
All through the world, blind unbelief's in power?
It rushes on and rules the present hour;
    Against Thy name!

Hell's gates are opened wide, and storming,
Through the tides of life's dull fate;

Man seeks to lead the masses of mankind
By selfish tyranny and bitter hate,
    Not in Thy name.

His better aspirations pale beneath
The weight of life's ambitions;
Come to the rescue, Lord; Thy wisdom give
To man, Thy wonderful creation,
    In Thine own name.

CLING NOT TO THE PAST.

"LET the dead past bury its dead,"
  The poet said;
And there rolled from off the living present
A weight of memories, that were heavy
With all that makes life scarcely worth the living, —
Long remembered heartaches, when friendship's flowers
Were crushed beneath the feet of some daring soul,
Who, wanting power, cared not for the wrecks it wrought,
So that the goal it sought and struggled for was gained.
It is hard to see our own fond hopes and
Aspirations thus trampled in the dust, —

The love of friends, once golden and sincere,
Through some unkind thought, or word let drop,
Forever turned upon you with reserve;
But, hard as this may be to bear, I would
Not be the soul to share the memories
That must come and go within the wake
Of such ambitions at last realized.
So, "Let the dead past bury its dead."
And soon the ghosts of many deeds undone,
The hosts of opportunities now lost,
The golden moments of forgotten purposes, —
Often returning in their fevered tread,
To crush the soul in deepest agony, —
Will pass away forever,
And all life's work, forgiven its mistakes,
Will be accepted for its worth.

QUESTIONINGS.

OH, weary soul !
    Why dost thou question the Lord's decrees?
Why look'st thou for subtle powers,
Ruling this wondrous world of ours?

Dost thou not know,
Canst thou not feel, within thy breast,
A will that governs thy behests,
An anchorage thy love attests?

Dost thou not see,
Not here to mortals is it given
To know the mysteries of earth,
Or solve the mystery of birth?

Hast thou not felt,
When trials prest upon thy heart,
When the soul with joy expands,
Infinite power thy will commands?

Curb not thy life,
With immortality endowed;
Crush not its hidden deeper springs;
Give full weight to all it brings.

Live close to Christ;
Who ever dwells anear to Him,
Forever banishes from life
The fretting cares of deadly strife.

IN THE END.

WHY the trials,
Why the passions,
Why the daily contradictions of the human soul?
Like waves dashing, forces clashing,
Courage giving to the living,
Thus through much of tribulation seek life's goal;
Richer will be the spirit's growth, greater its worth,
In the end.

Is the conflict
Worth the struggle?
Are life's purposes so weak that we the question dare?
Light is breaking, right is gaining;
Might is greater, fight the better.

When more fierce the battle rages, the greater care;
But character will ripen fast, and by it gain,
    In the end.

    Oft repenting,
    Often falling;
This is our life's great undertaking, to retain
    All the goodness and the gladness,
    In the building of our being;
Striving thus creation's greatest purpose to attain,
To become what God Himself designed, that we
    should be
    In the end.

SHIELDING.

"Oh that I could shield our children from the storms and vexatious trials of the world!"

I WOULD not shield them if I could,
    These pledges of our love,
From all the ills and woes of life,
    Assigned by God above.

Out in the world's great paths of right
    They're treading not alone;
Beneath the Artist's chisel-work
    Doth all creation moan.

For not in days of greatest ease
    Will we best treasure find;
The roughest paths and sternest needs
    Create the strongest mind;

Create the longings of the soul,
   Which find no answer here,
Save in the loving heart's embrace,
   Of Christ our Saviour near.

Then welcome them, our children dear,
   Trials as well as joy;
The outward strifes of daily life
   Will not the soul destroy.

But welcome them with trembling,
   Bespeak the Saviour's prayer,
That wheresoe'er the Father leads,
   To keep you in His care.

September 6, 1874.

SHADOWS.

WHY shrink we from the shadows,
    Which cross our steps at morn, —
The cool refreshing shadows,
    Forerunners of the dawn?

Why shrink we from the shadows,
    When comes the noontide heat, —
The daily lengthening shadows,
    Which bring us some retreat?

Why shrink we from the shadows,
    As eventide draws near, —
Those loving restful shadows,
    To weary ones most dear?

SHADOWS.

As taller grow the pine-trees,
   Within the densest shade,
So nobler grows the human soul,
   When on it cares are laid.

Why seek we always sunshine,
   Oh, spirit, tell me why?
No life's so full of sunshine
   But on it shadows lie.

No soul so free from sorrow,
   But sometime, on its brow,
Will sit serene the sorrow
   That's christening it now.

December 25, 1878.

"REST FOR THE WEARY."

AND must it always be my cross, to bear
    Life's joys and pleasures, sorrows and the like,
        With weary care?
If thus, why do I mourn? for it is said:
    "Bring all our cares to Him who for us careth;
Lay all our burdens down, for still He beareth."

And so it is, when on Christ's loving breast
    I rest my weary head and say, "Thou knowest;
        Forgive me, lest
I murmur or repine," life does not seem
    The heavy cross it did at early morn,
For at His feet I've laid my burdens down.

EASTER BELLS.

HEAR the Easter bells all ringing;
　　Listen to their message bringing
Bethlehem's glad song again, —
" Peace on earth, good-will to men."
On the wings of fleetest dawning,
In the early gray of morning,
Angels speed with loving hands,
To unloose death's tightened bands.

Such the mission of the angels.
This the story of the annals,
Soldier guards are wrapped in slumber;
Not a soul of all their number
Hears the Easter bells all ringing,
Hears the heavenly chorus singing,

"On earth peace, good-will to men;
Christ, our Lord, is risen again."

But while Easter bells are ringing,
Mary's to the garden bringing
Balm and spices in her hand,
To fulfil her heart's command.
Other women there are watching,
Waiting for the glorious morning,
When the Christ, at early dawn,
Seals the resurrection morn.

LIGHT AHEAD.

NOT so dark the pathway, darling,
    Light ahead ! we cry.
Jesus lifts the darkest clouds,
    That before us lie, —

Lifts and shows the future brighter;
    We cannot deny,
It is better, better far, to
    Know the truth than die.

To know the truth and struggle well
    For the health we need,
Shows a greater confidence
    In our Saviour's lead

Than dying, as our fondest hopes
   Are blossoming so fair.
Thank God! He seals our stewardship,
   Marks our daily care,

Accepts the labor and the life,
   We would gladly give,
To bring our children, day by day,
   Nearer the Christ to live.

GUIDANCE.

THOU leadest me, so great the thought,
    So full of inspiration wrought,
It fills my soul; naught e'er betides,
When in such faith my soul abides.

Thou leadest me, though dark the way;
My feet shall never from Thee stray;
For when I walk, my hand in Thine,
I feel Thy presence all divine.

Thou leadest me; and that is best,
Though disappointments fill my breast.
Though earthly aspirations fail,
Thou leadest to the "Holy Grail."

Thou leadest me; the day grows short,
The night comes onward; and apart
From all the surging cares of life,
From all its labor and its strife,

Thou leadest me through death's dark night;
Thou leadest me to realms of light;
Thus gathered in Thine arms to rest,
My longing soul is truly blest.

TO MY MOTHER.

SHE builded better than she knew,
    Gates of pearl and crystal dew,
Arching high above her head,
In the way the Father led.

She builded better than she knew,
Walls of sapphire's varied hue,
Flashing far, through sin's dark night,
Brilliant rays from God's own light.

She builded better than she knew,
When, with lavish hand and true
Scattering kind deeds everywhere,
Lifting many a weight of care.

TO MY MOTHER.

She builded better than she knew,
When, from hidden depths, she drew
Words of love, in kindness spoken,
Falling from her lips in token

Of the dear Saviour's presence there,
Beaming in her face so fair,
Dwelling in her soul divine,
Precious tabernacle thine.

She builded thus, till life was o'er,
Till, within the open door,
Heard she the glad song of love,
Calling to the home above.

A FAREWELL.

IT was a day of summer's sunshine without,
    But within hearts were shadowed with parting,
For mother was gently passing away
To the great " Beyond," as the night to day.
Her soul, gladdened with its near fruition
Of things unseen to our mortal vision,
Looked out upon us, with its quiet peace,
With its loving, longing benediction.
And thus she spake:
" In the Lord put all thy trust, my children;
No good thing will He withhold from those
Who rest within the fold of His great heart,
So strong to bear your spirits, so willing
To share your very heaviest crosses,

Or to relieve your very lightest care.
Trust Him for more than e'en your daily bread;
Trust Him for your soul's real life instead !
But knowing this,
That wheresoe'er the Father leads is best,
More bravely can you do your life's work well.
When called to drink the cup of bitter-sweet
That is so often pressed to human lips,
Search for hidden meaning in its depths,
More oft the bitterness will be most kind.
Or if you see the brighter ray that lines
The darkest cloud that overhangs your path,
Most gladly will your hearts in earnest say,
'Our God is King, and kind is all His way;'
If you can feel, as Jesus felt that night
Of sacrifice, 'Thy will, not mine is best,'
It will color all your daily inner life
With one sweet thought: it is the Christ
Who is leading me to-day. And though no

Open door we find away from burdens,
Every gate 's ajar, and every one swings far,
Where Christ an entrance gains; we may follow,
If we will, the footsteps of the Master."
Thus ended the loving benediction
Of the last evening hour, " Mother's farewell."

August, 1873.

INTO THE SILENCE.

INTO the silence come apart,
    My soul, and rest awhile,
For the great eternal silence
    Will keep thee free from guile.
Into the stillness turn aside
    From bustling cares of life,
The great eternal stillness,
    So free from mortal strife.

Within the presence of thy Lord,
    Seek constantly to be ;
The great eternal Presence,
    Awaits, my soul, for thee.

Drink from the living fountain-spring
    Of God's eternal truth,
And in the living pastures green,
    Immortalize thy youth.

Creative energies combine
    In everything that lives;
Creative force is in His hand,
    Which He most freely gives.
Then come into His presence, come,
    Fear not, His love receive:
The promises are infinite
    To all who will believe.

"Ask, I will give eternal life;"
    Ye cannot ask in vain.
"As is thy day, thy strength shall be,"
    And great shall be thy gain.

Eternal life, eternal strength,
   To meet each daily need,
It were well at times to turn aside,
   Upon such truths to feed.

June, 1894.

WITHERED LEAVES.

HEAR Thou my prayer to-night:
    Let not life's withered leaves
In any year to come behold the light.

The lessons they have taught
Thou knowest, Lord, full well
Have been well learned, or else their work was lost.

Too late, too late, those dead,
Dead leaves to rake, and hope
For aught but bitterness of them to make.

Buried beneath the snows
Of many a winter's frost,
No better spot can be for withered leaves.

CHRISTMAS' AMEN.

MAY a Merry, Merry Christmas
    Dawn on your path to-day,
Filling your heart with gladness,
    With many a merry lay.

And when the day is ended,
    And business rules again,
May there follow in its wake
    This Christmas' Amen.

December 25, 1875.

THE DYING YEAR.

THE year grows cold
As age o'er ages fold;
The same sad tale is told, —
The year grows cold.
So dark the night!
Oh, morning, bring the light!
The year is shorn of might,
At dead of night,

But not of love;
For, in God's house above,
Is nestled, like a dove,
The year's great love, —
The joys she brought,
The daily deeds she wrought,

The perfect love that sought
A life full-fraught

For every one:
Until the battle's won.
Until life's work is done,
For every one.
These are the sheaves
Of daily ripened leaves;
Most gladly Christ receives
These garnered sheaves.

With love and fear,
We mourn the old year sere.
Why grieve me? cries the year,
Why weep ye here?
Why mourn the past?
The present will not last;
The future travels fast
Into the past.

Let midnight fall;
A glory lifts the pall.
" Happy New Year " to all,
The new hopes call.
" Happy New Year "
Re-echoes far and near,
Inspires all hearts with cheer.
God bless the year!

OAKLAND, CALIFORNIA,
    New Year's Eve,
        1876.

*AS joined our hearts in labor,
   So join our hands in play,
And rend all care asunder,
   On this our festal day.
Too few our days of pleasure,
   Too few our hours of rest,
While one in our endeavor
   To do our level best.*

HOLIDAYS OF 1873.

To the Children:

IT is the night after New Year's;
　The guests have departed,
　Half the children have flown;
The house seems deserted;
　We are left alone.
Sweet Herbert, the baby,
　With cunningest air;
And Bessie, the honest child,
　Truthful and fair;
With Arthur and Willie, —
　No more do we see
Their bright happy faces,
　Nor list to their glee.
A week of hilarity,

Skating, sliding, and fun,
 Was there ever such sport,
  Since their world was begun?
It was Santa Claus' business,
 Upon last Christmas night,
To hide all the stockings,
 His special delight.
So he bent to the task
 With a hearty good-will,
As fast as the mothers
 The stockings could fill.
A six-footer's overcoat
 Hung in the hall,
With pockets so ample,
 Into one he let fall
A stocking crammed full,
 Till the goodies o'errun,
And laughed in his sleeve
 To think of the fun;

Kindling and shavings
  Covered one in the grate.
"What a joke," thought Saint Nick,
  "Should a little boy take
A match and set fire
  To his candies and cake."
They were tied to the table legs,
  Tucked into drawers,
Packed into clothes-baskets,
  And thrown behind doors.
Then orders, " No mouthful
  Of food in the morn,
Until each little child
  Brings his stocking along."
So, nine little children,
  Who were packed off to beds
At eight in the evening,
  Were showing their heads
At six in the morning,

And this was their song:
"Merry Christmas to all;
  Bring your stocking along."
There were searchings and
  Huntings, and screams of delight
As one and another
  Brought something to light.
One poor little waif,
  I think it was Birdie,
Sought all through the house,
  From story to story, —
"Where could old Saint Nick
  Have hidden the thing?
Not a mouthful of food
  Till it I can bring."
I know that she found it,
  For breakfast was gay:
That Christmas will cheer us
  For many a day.

A VALENTINE.

LILIES, roses,
    Sweetest posies,
For my little ones to-day;
    Skies the brightest,
    Hearts the lightest,
Life, one blooming year of May.

    If a cloud, a
    Silver lining
Turns its brightness to your sight;
    If a shower,
    And sun is shining,
There will be a rainbow bright.

If a storm of
Wind is blowing,
And the thunders heavy crash,
Soon will come the
Pouring raindrops,
And the lightning's vivid flash.

If it is night,
The pale moonlight
Will watch over while you sleep;
And may God's peace,
His joy o'ershine
And all your hearts from evil keep!

LITTLE CHILDREN.

LITTLE children, flocked together
    In life's garden, by the way,
Come, and let me ask you kindly,
    What you 're thinking as you play?

Have you thought your pastimes, even,
    Formed a scaffolding so rare,
That by them you 're mounting upward,
    If you watch your feet with care?

Have you thought the cross word spoken,
    Coming quickly to your lips,
Leaves its impress on your spirit,
    If beyond the tongue it slips?

Thought how full of joy is childhood?
When your little spirit swells
Only with the happiest feelings,
Life is full of asphodels.

Thought how swiftly days are fleeting,
And the years come on apace?
Keep your hearts, then, pure and simple
To be ready for life's race.

AN APRIL DAY.

"Ah, my little Baby Bay,
 Where are you this April day?
The flowers have come,
The birds now sing,
The air is full of living things;
And *you*, my blithesome Baby Bay,
What do you, this April day?"

"Like the bee upon the wing,
Gath'ring honey while I sing,
Playing out among the flowers,
All the livelong happy hours,
I'll pick up pleasures as they drop,
To fill my cup full to the top,
Then I'll lay me down to rest,

When the dusky shades of night
Draw a curtain o'er my sight."

" Baby Bay, what seest thou,
In the beauty of the flower,
In all things so full of life?
Tell me, Bay, what dost thou hear
In the song-bird's notes so clear,
In the humming of the bees,
In the rustling of the trees?"

" Mother dear, a hand I see,
Leading you and leading me,
All things richly to enjoy,
Is the music that I hear,
Thrilling all the world with cheer;
Do not call me from my play
On this lovely April day."

17 La Fayette Place, *April* 27, 1879.

BABY ADALYN.

BABY Adalyn is a beauty,
    With her curly locks of gold;
Her laughing eyes of sunny blue
    The deepest wealth of love can hold.

Her lips the morning sun has kissed,
    And giv'n a touch of rosy hue
To all her features, born so fair,
    Fresh as the morning's breath of dew.

Her very form is full of love,
    As, holding you in warm embrace,
It gives you more than you can ask
    Of the true lover's hidden grace.

But would you see our Golden Locks
    Filled full of nature's sweet content,
Then watch her with four kittens small,
    Upon their gambols all intent.

Cooing, kissing, fondling, hugging,
    Hear her calling with delight,
" You pretty, pretty little dears ; "
    There never was a sweeter sight.

SQUIBNOCKET, *August*, 1894.

BABY BELLE HINCHLIFF.

"What are you doing, Grandmamma?" "I am painting your picture." "Oh!"

THE winsomest child that ever was seen,
  Is our dainty baby Belle.
The sky's own blue is in her eyes,
Heaven's own sunshine in her hair;
Her teeth like pearls from out the sea,
Her lips two rubies, pigeon red;
Her cheeks two roses pink and white,
Her ears two coral shells;
Two beautiful arms surround our necks
With tender love's encircling grace;
Two beautiful feet to do our bidding;
Two beautiful hands to her are given
Ours to hold within their grasp;

Her form is full of life and ease ;
But greater far than the body fair
Is the beautiful soul that is treasured there.
She speaks to us of love as true,
As the love of hearts God's will to do ;
And we wonder why to this world of care,
Has come such a dear little spirit rare.

July 8, 1894.

KISSES.

DEAR little children, kisses so sweet
    Come in your letters my life to greet.
One, two, three, four pulls, that's how we tell
When it's the mail-man rings the doorbell.

Knapsack he carries, trudges along,
Leaving the letters till all are gone;
Comes in the morning, noon, and at night;
Uncle Sam's gentleman does it all right.

WATCHING FOR MAMMA.

BABY, looking out for me,
    Claps her hands with joyous glee,
And we hear her glad refrain,
" Mamma's coming home again."
Dearest music for the soul
Do these little songsters hold ;
Sweetest mysteries of life,
    They to us unfold.

Happy darling ! Do you hear?
Birds are singing very near,
Thoughts of home within stirring,
Thoughts of loved ones are bringing
Joy and gladness to my life,
Which is full of earnest strife ;
And trembling with a deep delight,
Is my heart to-night.

TO THE LINNET.

LINNET! linnet!
　　Wait a minute,
I have searched for you all day;
　　Heard you singing
　　In the thicket:
Come and tell me where you stay.

　　Sweetest singer,
　　In the tree-tops,
Show your pretty nest to me;
　　I shall not rob you,
　　I shall not harm you,
I shall not steal your eggs to see.

I will protect you,
I will love you,
Oh, my pretty linnet gay;
Sing your sweetest
Lays and ditties,
To amuse me while at play.

SQUIBNOCKET.
For Ralph Thompson, at his request.

THE DIAMOND NECKLACE.

TWO loving little maidens sat,
    Upon a summer's day;
Before them on a velvet cushion,
    A diamond necklace lay.

They looked upon its beauty rare
    With long admiring gaze,
Marking its brilliant scintillations,
    Its bright reflected rays.

"Oh, when I am a woman grown,
    Such jewels will I wear,"
Said one. The other, "Oh, that I
    Had jewels still more fair!"

In the darkening, deepening twilight,
    Of a cold winter's day,
Two women sat in love's embrace,
    Recounting life's long way, —

The one in robe of ermine fur,
    With jewels rich and rare;
The other in her plain attire,
    No jewels, but so fair.

They talked of their ambitions once,
    Upon that summer day,
When sparkling to their youthful eyes,
    The diamond necklace lay.

"So great were my desires once,
    For jewels were my joy,
But oh, how they have tarnished, since
    Possession can destroy."

" 'T is true I longed for jewels, too,
    But asked for some more fair;
Richer gifts were then bestowed,
    Through children's loving care."

A JINGLE.

JINGLE ! jingle !
Dingle ! dingle !
Sings this little head of mine.
Baby loves it ;
Baby wants it ;
Baby is my valentine.

Listen, pretty !
To my ditty,
It is written for a dime ;
If the jingle,
And the dingle,
Suit your fancy, you are mine.

For Baby Adalyn.

LAMBKIN.

THE lambkin's bleat! bleat!
　　Comes up from the fold:
"Oh, mamma, where are you?
　　I am very cold."

The old sheep's baa! baa!
　　Comes back to the lamb:
"Oh, come to me, dearest;
　　I'll snuggle you warm."

NATURE'S UNDERTONES.

THERE is music everywhere;
    Floating in the balmy air,
Where the melody of praise
Can its sweetest notes upraise;
Dwelling in the summer breeze,
These are its soliloquies:
"Trust your pretty leaves to me,
To make music o'er the lea;
I will clap their hands for joy
In a world of song."

Music, when the Autumn flower
Yields to frost its brilliant dower
Dropping from the parent stem,
Singing its own requiem,

Floating, floating down to lie
At the feet of trees to die,
Coming from the little rill
As it tumbles down the hill,
On its gambols free and wild,
Merry as a child.

Music in the rolling spheres,
As they travel through the years
Scattering, from their starry light,
Brightness through the darkest night;
Till each ray a brilliant note
Can our happiness promote;
No sweeter anthem, we confess,
Than the music stars possess,
Mingling with the pale moon's ray
Night's sweet roundelay.

List the music of the snow
Gently falling, soft and low;

Sweet the strains its voices give,
Singing, singing we shall live,
To the thirsty earth restore
Budding, blooming time once more.
Music children love to hear,
Ringing through the air so clear,
Is the jingling sleigh-bells' chime
And the crackling rime.

E'en all harsh disturbing noise
Vibrates with a certain poise,
Some rich strains the heart will fill
That is music's best idyl;
Though some notes are harsh, severe,
They make the harmony appear.
Yield yourself to be caressed
By music not in words expressed,
For the rhythmic waves of sound
Everywhere abound.

Oh, the musical breath of the air,
    And the musical rush of the sea,
And the musical whirr of things unseen,
    All are sounding an anthem to me.

Note the whistling in tops of the pines,
    With the rustling of beautiful leaves;
All the rhythmical voice of the winds
    Into wonderful song interweaves.

THE FUTURE.

"OF what are you thinking, little mother,
    As back to my studies I go?
Tell me your thoughts, the moments are fleeting,
    That bear me away *de novo*."

"I am thinking, my boy, of your future;
    The present, so joyously full,
Giving promise of all that is noble,
    If the right you never annul.

"I am thinking how quickly this future
    Will bring you life's duties to face;
Added to courage that knowledge can give,
    There must be a heart full of grace.

"I am thinking the almanac's record
    Will mark many days in their flight,
Ere again we sit down thus together,
    And talk of our love as to-night.

"So I leave you, my boy, to your study,
    Though evil is everywhere rife,
And pray God to bless you and guide you
    In planning and training for life."

THE END.

THE PRINTING WAS DONE BY
JOHN WILSON AND SON AT THE
UNIVERSITY PRESS IN CAMBRIDGE
UNDER THE DIRECTION OF
STONE AND KIMBALL OF CHICAGO
THE SEVENTH OF SEPTEMBER
M D CCC XC IV

www.ingramcontent.com/pod-product-compliance
Lightning Source LLC
Chambersburg PA
CBHW020238170426

43202CB00008B/130